D0997716

Shipbuilding

James L Wood

NMS Publishing

Published by NMS Publishing, Chambers Street, Edinburgh EHI IJF

© James L Wood & Trustees of the National Museums of Scotland 1998

Series Editor Iseabail Macleod

British Library Cataloguing in Publication Data

A catalogue record of this book is available from the British Library

ISBN 0 948636 95 5

Series design by NMS Publishing Ltd, designed by Janet Watson

Printed in Great Britain by Cambridge University Press Printing Division

Acknowledgements

The assistance of the following individuals and institutions is gratefully acknowledged by
the author. Staff of the Library and the Department of Science, Technology and Working
Life, National Museums of Scotland; John Edwards, Aberdeen Maritime Museum;
Janette Archibald, Alloa Museum; Ian Murray, Clackmannanshire Archieves, Alloa;
Niall MacNeill, Scottish Maritime Museum, Denny Tank, Dumbarton; Janice Murray,
McManus Galleries. Dundee; Veronica Hartwich, Scottish Maritime Museum, Irvine;
Jack Sanderson and Carol Sneddon, Callendar House Museum, Falkirk; Murdoch
Nicolson, Mitchell Library, Glasgow; Alastair Smith, Museum of Transport, Glasgow;
Gavin Grant, Kirkcaldy Museum & Art Gallery; Don Martin, William Patrick Library,
Kirkintilloch; Alan Macdonald, Crieff; John Porter, London; Gillian Wood; Andrew
Wood.

Illustrations: Front cover, 17, 69 bottom, 78: J L Wood. 4, 29: Kirkcaldy Museum and
Art Gallery. 8 top: National Gallery of Scotland. 8 bottom, 10, 12, 19, 22, 23, 45, 47, 49,
52, 57, 60, 66, 68, 69 top, 72, 74: National Museums of Scotland. 15: Reproduced with
permission of the Keeper of the Records of Scotland. UCS1/box326/no.9. 16: Summerlee
Heritage Trust. 20, 27: Aberdeen Art Gallery and Museums Collections. 21: San
Francisco Maritime Museum, per the Clyde Museum Trust. 25, 71: Courtesy of the
Mitchell Library, Glasgow City Libraries and Archives. 32: Scottish Maritime Museum,
Irvine. 35, 51, 70: Courtesy of John Hume. 37: Clackmannanshire Library Services. 39,
41: Ferguson Shipbuilders Limited. 44: Scottish National Portrait Gallery. 65: Dundee
City Council, Arts and Heritage Department. 75: Kvaerner Govan

Illustrations captioned SLA are from the Scottish Life Archive in the National Museums
of Scotland.

Front cover: *Transatlantic liner* Lucania *completed by Fairfield, at
Govan for Cunard in 1893.* The Campania, *illustrated on pp* 60,68-69
was a sister ship.

CONTENTS

INTRODUCTION

Ships have a special appeal and the Scottish shipbuilding industry at its peak aroused widespread interest. Among the people who built the ships there was a genuine pride in the industry and its products, despite the fact that they worked in appalling conditions in all weathers, with little reward or job security. They might therefore have been expected to have a less than romantic view. As one nineteenth-century naval architect, William John, put it:

> If any body of men have just cause to feel pride in their calling, and in the fruits of their labour, shipbuilders have. If we look at the magnitude of the operations of building, launching, engining, and completing a modern passenger ship of the first rank, and regard the multiplicity of the arrangements and beauty of finish now expected, and then think this structure has to brave the elements, make regular passages, convey thousands of human souls, and tens of thousands of tons of merchandise every year across the ocean, in storm or calm, we cannot but feel that they are occupied in useful human labour.

Ships are isolated self-contained communities and before the coming of radio they were cut off from the world for days, or even months. It is this isolation which gives rise to the romantic view of the ship. Even with modern communications and navigational aids the sense of detachment from the world is still present.

This book is concerned with the birth, growth and subsequent decline of one of Scotland's most important industries of the nineteenth and early twentieth centuries. Although the early history is touched on, the main concern is with the transition

The high point of the shipbuilding process, the successful launch of the Burntisland-built motor ship Bosworth, *18 February 1946.*

from wood and sail to iron (and steel) and steam. Accompanying these technical changes there was the transformation of shipbuilding from a small-scale affair meeting local needs, into a large-scale industrialized process which led the world in the production of ships for customers throughout Britain and the rest of the world. However, this was a transient glory and the decline of the industry in Scotland is also charted. Unfortunately there is not space to cover every aspect of the shipbuilding industry and the emphasis has had to be on the building of sea-going merchant ships and warships, rather than small craft such as fishing boats and pleasure boats.

The size and complexity of the industry was such that only an outline, and largely non-technical, history is possible. It is centred on the work of some of the bigger and better-known shipbuilding firms and the people connected with them, but these represent only a fraction of the total number of firms involved in the industry. Over a period of 200 years there were more than 250 shipbuilders on the Clyde alone, many of them short-lived. Between them they built a total of around 30,000 ships of many different types. As well as the large liners which most people associate with the Clyde shipyards, there were smaller passenger ships, cargo liners, cross-channel ferries, tramp steamers, sailing ships, tugs, dredgers, and warships of all kinds from battleships to submarines. In addition, although overshadowed by the Clyde, there was a significant shipbuilding industry on the east coast of Scotland.

For readers looking for additional information there are suggestions for further reading. Information is also given about museums with shipbuilding material and about historic ships open to visitors.

In dealing with an industry such as shipbuilding the use of technicalities is difficult to avoid completely. One of the most confusing terms is 'tonnage' which can be used in several different ways and some explanation seems called for here. In this book it is used only to refer to the 'gross tonnage' of a merchant ship.

This has nothing to do with weight but is a measure of the internal volume of a ship, calculated on the basis that one hundred cubic feet (2.832 cubic metres) equals one ton. The gross tonnage represents the total internal volume and is therefore an indicator of the size of a ship. From the gross tonnage the volume of certain areas essential for the operation of the ship, such as the machinery spaces, is deducted to give the net tonnage. The net figure is of great importance to the shipowner as it is used to calculate various charges such as harbour dues. Note that the modern metric equivalent of gross tonnage is calculated on a completely different basis and conversion from one to the other is not possible. The other tonnage figures which can be used are 'displacement' which is simply the weight of water displaced by the ship and hence, by the principle of Archimedes, the weight of the ship and its contents and 'deadweight' which is the weight of cargo carried. The displacement tonnage is most commonly used for warships, while the deadweight is given for ships such as oil tankers and bulk ore or grain carriers. Both these are measured in tons and can be converted to metric tons, or tonnes, of 1,000 kilograms. One ton equals 1.016 tonnes.

Henry Bell (1767-1830), the first commercial steamboat operator in Europe.

Bell's paddle steamer Comet, *which went into service between Glasgow and Greenock in 1812.*

SHIPBUILDING

1 Scotland Supreme

With many navigable rivers, an indented coastline and numerous obstacles to movement overland, water transport was of vital importance to the early inhabitants of Scotland. The remains of many examples of boats made by hollowing out single logs have been found. One found near Locharbriggs, in Dumfriesshire, has been dated to around 1,800 BC, using the radio-carbon method. This is one of the earliest of those boats found in Britain which it has been possible to date with some confidence. The technique of making log boats was long-lived, other examples having been found in Britain from as late as the fourteenth century.

Boats made from a light framework covered with skins were probably more widely used than log boats. They would have been more fragile and therefore relatively short-lived, but set against this the construction of replacements would have been quick and less labour-intensive.

Vessels were being built in Scotland from the earliest times but these were small craft. They could be constructed on any piece of ground with access to water and a convenient supply of timber. The earliest reference to a site which could properly be called a shipyard, in the sense that it was equipped for the construction of sizeable sea-going vessels and was in use for a period of years, is not found until the early sixteenth century. This was the royal dockyard set up at Newhaven, on the Forth, as a result of the naval ambitions of King James IV. From Newhaven, in 1511, there emerged the *Great Michael*. At about 240 ft (73 m) in length, this was larger than any ship previously constructed in Scotland and had few equals anywhere. It was built at a time of great tension in relations between Scotland and England, which ended in the disastrous defeat of the Scots and the death of the King at the Battle of Flodden in 1513. The construction of this large and heavily armed warship, no doubt intended as the 'ultimate deterrent' of its time, was something of a leap in the dark as a shipbuilding project.

The *Great Michael* remained exceptional. Until the end of the eighteenth century ships built in Scotland were of much more modest size and were constructed to meet local demand for fishing boats and coastal traders. The main shipbuilding centres

Conjectural model of the Great Michael, *completed at Newhaven on the Forth in 1511, for the navy of King James IV.*

were on the east coast and it was only around Greenock and Dumbarton that there was much activity in the west. Although Scottish trade with America, particularly the importing of tobacco, grew rapidly in the eighteenth century and made large fortunes for a small number of Glasgow merchants, most of it was carried on in American-built ships. In the next century the Clyde was to dominate the industry, not only in Scottish but also in British and in world terms.

The development of the steamship began in Scotland with the experiments of Patrick Miller of Dalswinton (1731-1815), a landowner and banker from Dumfriesshire, James Taylor who was employed by Miller as a tutor for his son, and William Symington, the engineer at the Wanlockhead lead mines. There has been much debate concerning the relative importance of the contribution of these three but what is clear is that in October 1788 an experimental steamboat fitted with an engine built by Symington was tried, with some success, on Dalswinton Loch, on Miller's estate. In 1800 Symington obtained backing from the Forth & Clyde Canal Company for work on an experimental steamboat intended as a possible replacement for the horses used to tow canal boats. The boat was built by Alexander Hart of Grangemouth and fitted with an engine designed by Symington. Trials took place on the canal in 1801 and were reasonably successful. A second and improved boat, probably with the same engine, was launched in 1802 and tested early in the following year, proving capable of towing two canal boats a distance of eighteen and a half miles in nine and a quarter hours. This was the well-known *Charlotte Dundas*, named after the daughter of Lord Dundas, the Governor of the Forth & Clyde Canal Company. There was no doubt that steamboats could be made to work, although the company, concerned about the expense and possible damage to the banks of the canal, was unwilling to proceed any further.

Although Symington's work had shown that a practical steamboat could be built, it was left to the American, Robert Fulton, to build the first one to be used on a commercial service. Fulton had

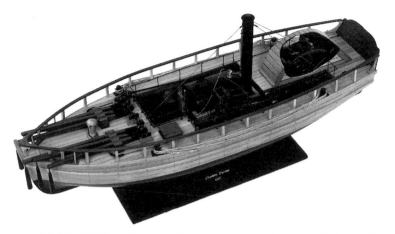

Model of William Symington's steam tug for the Forth & Clyde Canal, the Charlotte Dundas, *completed in 1802. It worked well but the Canal Company decided not to continue the experiment.*

met Symington and seen the *Charlotte Dundas* after the end of the 1803 trials. When he returned to America he built the *Clermont* and in 1807, on the Hudson River, he started the world's first commercial steamboat service.

Another man who saw the *Charlotte Dundas*, was Henry Bell, millwright, builder, property developer and proprietor of a hotel in Helensburgh, on the Clyde. When Henry Bell decided to have a steamship built he was aware of what had been done by Symington and Fulton and would therefore have been in no doubt that these new contraptions could be made to work. In the rapidly developing industrial west of Scotland the essential elements of a steamboat were readily obtainable. There were experienced builders of wooden hulls on the lower reaches of the Clyde and the new power-driven cotton-spinning industry in and around Glasgow had given rise to steam-engine and boiler-making firms. The development of a commercial steamboat only needed someone who had a use for one, and could scheme out something incorporating the various elements of the existing technology. That said, it was still a big step in the dark and required much courage.

In 1811 Henry Bell placed the order with the shipbuilder John Wood & Company of Port Glasgow for the forty-three and a half feet (thirteen metre) long vessel *Comet*, with an engine by John Robertson of Glasgow and a boiler by David Napier, also of Glasgow. Apart from a long-standing interest in the possibilities of steam navigation Bell had a quite specific need for a vessel. He wanted to increase the number of people patronizing his Helensburgh hotel, the Baths Inn, by providing better transport from Glasgow. The *Comet* made its 20 mile (32 km) delivery voyage from Port Glasgow to the Broomielaw quay, Glasgow, on 6 August 1812, taking three and a half hours. A few days later a regular thrice-weekly service was begun between Glasgow and Greenock, passengers for Helensburgh being served by a connecting sailing vessel.

The relative merits of the various pioneers of steam navigation have been the subject of considerable debate over the years. What is beyond dispute is that Henry Bell, certainly building on the work of others (and this is how virtually all new things are created), was able to put together all the elements necessary for the creation of the first commercial steamer service in Europe. The time was right, technically and commercially, and within twenty years there were fifty-nine steamers in service on the Clyde. In addition a considerable number had been built on the river for coastal and short sea routes elsewhere.

The rise of Scotland, and of the Clyde in particular, as the centre of excellence in world shipbuilding was founded on the development of the steamship as a practical and commercially viable means of transport. It was the engineers who led the building of the new steamships, rather than the old-established builders of wooden ships. Of these early engineers the greatest were Robert and David Napier. Robert combined engineering talent with the ability to pick the right men to help him and a flair for business. His cousin David was perhaps more innovative as an engineer but lacked the commercial ability. A measure of their importance is that of the fifty-nine ships noted above, sixteen had engines by David Napier and eleven by Robert.

Contributing much to the success of Robert Napier's firm and illustrating his talent for picking the right man for the job was David Elder, a brilliant but little-known engineer who started working for Robert Napier shortly before 1823, when he began to build marine engines. In time Elder's role grew in importance and he became responsible for the high standards of engine design and construction which gave the firm its great reputation for technical quality. Coupled with Robert Napier's commercial ability and skill in making and keeping the contacts with customers, this was the foundation of the firm's success.

Engines were built for many vessels for operation on the Clyde but, as steamships came to be widely accepted and their capabilities appreciated, both Napiers began to build engines for ships engaged in, for example, services between Scotland and Ireland, and coastal services from Scottish ports to London. In 1836 Robert Napier secured an order from the Honourable East India Company for the *Berenice*, his first ocean-going ship. This was completed in the following year and made an uneventful voyage to Bombay, to the great satisfaction of the East India Company and the commander, Captain Grant. In 1838, Napier received his first order from the Admiralty, for machinery for two naval vessels which were being built in the dockyards. The year 1838 also saw the Admiralty inviting tenders for the provision of a transatlantic mail service by steamer. The contract was won by Samuel Cunard of Halifax, Nova Scotia, who then set up the British & North American Royal Mail Steam Packet Company to operate the service. The company ordered four ships from Robert Napier and the service began on 4 July 1840, when the paddle steamer *Britannia* left Liverpool for Boston.

Robert Napier was still only a builder of machinery, but the importance of the machinery at this stage in the development of

Robert Napier's Lancefield engine works, Glasgow, on the north bank of the Clyde. The ship is Cunard's last wooden paddle steamer Arabia *which was completed in 1852.*

the steamship is reflected in the fact that in the case of the *Berenice* and the vessels for Cunard, and many others, Napier was the main contractor. He undertook to supply the complete ship and sub-contracted the work of building the hull. These early vessels were all wooden paddle steamers but great changes were on the way. Iron shipbuilding and screw propulsion were coming.

The first iron vessel of any sort is believed to have been a canal boat built in 1787 by the English ironmaster, John Wilkinson. The first in Scotland was the *Vulcan*, a horse-drawn canal boat for passenger service on the Forth & Clyde Canal. This was completed in 1819 by Thomas Wilson at Faskine, near Airdrie, on the Monkland Canal. It must have given satisfaction, despite the use of a new and untried material, as it was not broken up until

Modern replica of the first iron vessel built in Scotland, the horse-drawn canal boat Vulcan. This was completed in 1819 at Faskine near Airdrie, on the Monkland Canal, for service on the Forth & Clyde Canal.

1873. In 1827 David Napier built an iron vessel for service on Loch Eck. Four years later the first iron ship to sail on the Clyde, the *Fairy Queen*, was built in Glasgow by John Neilson. The first Clyde shipyard specially laid out for the construction of iron vessels was that of Tod & MacGregor. They began as marine engineers in 1834 and expanded into shipbuilding within a few years, creating a new yard at Meadowside, Partick, on the north bank of the river.

Tod & Macgregor's yard was the first of many iron shipyards. In 1841 Robert Napier began iron shipbuilding on the south side of the Clyde, at Govan, so that he did not have to sub-contract the hulls of the ships for which he received orders. The first ship was completed in 1843. Among the notable ships built in Napier's Govan yard was the *Black Prince* (1861), the sister ship of the first ironclad, *Warrior*. Further armoured warships were built for both British and foreign navies. Among the overseas orders were three ships for the Turkish navy. The builder's model for one of them, the *Osman Ghazi* of 1864, is in the collection of the National Museums of Scotland. The merchant ships included Cunard's first iron vessel, the paddle steamer *Persia* of 1855, and their last paddle steamer *Scotia*, completed in 1862.

A consequence of the dominant position of Napier's firm in the important early decades of the industry was that many of the next generation of engineers and shipbuilders spent their formative years there as apprentices, journeymen, foremen and managers. There they learned their trade and learned it well. In 1879, the writer of an obituary notice for James R Napier, one of Robert Napier's sons, remarked that the works

> has a sort of classical history attaching to it as a great engineering school, in which the headmaster was not really Robert Napier, but David Elder, one of the most accomplished mechanics that ever held a place of trust in any workshop on the Clyde.

The launch of the Osman Ghazi *from the Govan shipyard of Robert Napier & Sons. This was one of three armoured warships completed in 1864 for the Turkish Government.*

Among those who passed through the Napier/Elder school were Charles Randolph, John Elder (son of David Elder), A C Kirk, William Denny (II), Walter Brock, and James and George Thomson. Their names make up a roll-call of leading Clyde shipbuilding personalities in the second half of the nineteenth century. They were young and willing to do things in new ways. The firms which they founded or managed competed strongly and effectively with their 'alma mater'.

The fact that a steamship could be made to work and run a commercial service on a river estuary was demonstrated by Henry Bell. Those who followed him, and especially David and Robert Napier, widened the scope of steamer operations to cover cross-channel and then trans-oceanic services. However the use of steam power was still limited because of high operating costs and the amount of space taken up by machinery and fuel. In the 1850s much the greater part of the world's trade was still carried by sailing ships which were significantly cheaper to operate than steamers. By then iron was becoming widely used and this made larger ships possible. The extra power needed for the larger ships was obtained simply by increasing the size of the engines and boilers. What was required was greater efficiency. In the next few decades new types of engines and boilers were developed, which took up less space, were lighter and used less coal. As a result, by the end of the nineteenth century, the operating costs of steamships had been reduced to a level at which large sailing ships for ocean trades could no longer compete. Most of the important developments were the result of the efforts of these Napier-trained engineers.

Charles Randolph started his business in Glasgow in 1834 as a millwright, supplying equipment for factories. In 1852 he was joined by John Elder and the firm, now called Randolph, Elder & Company, turned to marine engineering. As a millwright, Randolph was aware of well-proven developments in land engines which improved efficiency, and especially the use of 'compound' cylinders. These are of differing sizes and the steam is led first into the smaller of the two and then into the larger, before being condensed and returned to the boiler. This results in a significant reduction in steam consumption and hence fuel consumption compared with a 'simple' engine. In 1854 a ship called the *Brandon* was equipped with a compound engine, as a 'technology demonstrator', to use the modern term. The first order for a commercial installation was received in 1855. This came from the Pacific Steam Navigation Company for the engines for a new ship, the *Valparaiso*. The company operated on the west coast of South America where coal prices were high and therefore stood to benefit greatly from any increase in efficiency. They were well satisfied with the new ship. Further ships were built with compound engines and their existing vessels were sent back to Glasgow to have new compound engines installed. Randolph, Elder & Company were initially only engineers and did not begin shipbuilding until 1860. In later years

A C Kirk's triple-expansion engine installed in the SS Aberdeen *of 1881. The low fuel consumption of this type of engine eventually made the large ocean-going sailing ship uneconomical.*

they became John Elder & Company and then the Fairfield Shipbuilding and Engineering Company, one of the most famous names in Clyde shipbuilding history.

This process of improving the efficiency of the steam engine by compounding can be carried further by using the steam in three or four cylinders in succession, instead of just two. The three-stage or 'triple-expansion' engine was brought to fruition by Alexander C Kirk, who had started his apprenticeship with Napier in the mid 1840s. In 1872, by which time he was in charge of the engineering department at John Elder & Company, he designed a triple-expansion engine for the *Propontis*. Unfortunately, the ship incorporated another major innovation, high-pressure boilers of a novel design, which proved troublesome. It was not until 1881 that the new type of engine was given another chance. The *Aberdeen* was built by Robert Napier & Sons for the Aberdeen-based firm of G Thompson & Company. It proved to be a great success, being economical and reliable. Kirk was again responsible but by this time as a member of the partnership which had taken over Napier's firm in 1877, following the death of Robert Napier.

Associated with A C Kirk in the trials of the *Propontis* was Walter Brock, another ex-Napier apprentice. At the time of the *Propontis*

The SS Aberdeen, *was completed in 1881 by Robert Napier & Sons, Glasgow for the Aberdeen shipowner George Thompson.*

The Glenlee, *built of steel in 1896 by A Rodger & Company, Port Glasgow, represents the last generation of large sailing vessels. It is now being restored at Glasgow by the Clyde Maritime Trust.*

trials Brock was a partner in the shipbuilding firm of William Denny & Brothers and also of the associated engineering firm of Denny & Company. He was later to be one of the pioneers of the quadruple-expansion engine. This process of expanding the steam in a number of stages was subject to the law of diminishing returns. The benefits of compounding, or two-stage expansion, were very substantial. Triple-expansion usually gave a further worthwhile improvement, and it was the almost universal adoption of this type of engine which reduced the running cost of the steamship below that of the large ocean-going sailing ship. The additional gain from using four-stage expansion was fairly small and it was only used where the conditions were particularly suitable.

The name of Denny will always be associated with shipbuilding in Dumbarton. The first member of the family to have anything to do with shipbuilding, William Denny, built wooden ships from

Sectioned model of the Nerbudda, *of 1883, showing the compound engine and boilers as well as the structure of the hull. The ship was built for the British India Steam Navigation Company by William Denny & Brothers, Dumbarton. The model was made in the Museum's engineering workshop.*

1818-33. Three of his sons, led by William Denny (II), established the firm of Denny Brothers in 1844 to build iron ships. In 1849 the partnership was reorganized under the new name of William Denny & Brothers. They became one of the most innovative and successful of the Clyde shipbuilding firms, with a worldwide reputation for ships of high quality. They had a more scientific approach to ship design than most shipbuilders and they were pioneers in the systematic recording and evaluation of data from ship trials. In 1883 they brought into use a test tank in which scale models of hulls were towed at various speeds, and the resistance measured. It was the first tank of its kind to be built by a private shipbuilder anywhere in the world. With the benefit of the information derived from these tests the firm became the leading specialist builder of fast cross-channel ferries.

Two more ex-Napier men who gained great renown were James and George Thomson. When they set themselves up in business in 1847 they had been with Napier for about twenty years. At first they were marine engineers only, with a works in Glasgow known as the Clyde Bank Foundry. They began shipbuilding in Govan in 1851. In 1872 a move was made to a green-field site further down river, near Dalmuir, and both the shipyard and the community which grew up to house the workforce took the name of the original engine works, Clydebank. The firm came to specialize in large liners and warships, but orders for these were irregular and although they developed a first-class reputation it proved difficult to make a profit. In 1899 they were taken over by their largest creditor, the Sheffield steelmaker, John Brown & Company. As John Brown's they built for Cunard such famous ships as the *Lusitania*, *Aquitania*, *Queen Mary*, *Queen Elizabeth* and *Queen Elizabeth 2*. Few people now realize that the yard ever bore a name other than John Brown's.

So far, the developments discussed and the firms involved in them have been centred on the upper reaches of the Clyde, from Glasgow itself as far down river as Dumbarton. As already mentioned, Greenock and Port Glasgow were important centres in

Probably the most famous Clyde-built ship of all, the Queen Mary, *built for Cunard by John Brown & Company, Clydebank. Work started in 1930 but came to a standstill because both customer and builder were in financial difficulty. With Government assistance work was restarted in 1934. The ship was completed in 1936 and served until 1967. It is now a tourist attraction at Long Beach, California, USA.* SLA

earlier days for wooden shipbuilding. Of particular interest is the Greenock firm of Scott, founded in 1711. Long-established organizations, which have been become used to one kind of product and a particular type of technology, often fail to cope with fundamental changes in their industry. To every rule, however, there are exceptions and Scott's was one of these. They built their first steamers in 1815, buying engines from outside firms until, in 1825, an associated engineering firm, Scott, Sinclair & Company was set up to build engines for their ships. They also successfully made the transformation from wood to iron and in 1845 built an iron screw frigate for the Royal Navy. This was the start of a long naval connection which led, among other things, to the firm becoming one of the few with special expertise in the building of submarines. In complete contrast, in 1905 they turned out one of the last British-built ocean-going sailing cargo ships, the four-masted *Archibald Russell*.

A Greenock firm which, like Napier and several others on the upper reaches of the Clyde, came into shipbuilding via engineering, was Caird & Company. Their early history is obscure but they made the second engine to be installed in 1828 in the paddle steamer *Industry*. Built in 1814, and in operation until 1862, this was the longest-lived of the early steamers. Like Robert Napier they sometimes acted as the main contractor, building the engines themselves and sub-contracting the construction of the wooden hulls. Then in 1840 they took over the yard of one of the firms they employed as a sub-contractor and reorganized it to build iron ships. Their first iron vessel was completed in 1842.

Of a somewhat different character to Scott's and Caird's was the firm of Russell & Company, founded in Port Glasgow in 1874. The original partners were John Russell and Anderson Rodger but in 1882 when they took over the firm of Henry Murray & Company, also of Port Glasgow, they acquired not only another shipyard but some of the staff. Among them was chief draughtsman, William T Lithgow, who became a partner in Russell's. In 1891 the original partners departed and Lithgow took control. It

The Industry, *built at Fairlie by William Fife, was the longest lived of the early Clyde steamboats. Completed in 1814, only two years after the* Comet, *it remained in service until 1862.*

was not until 1918 that the name was changed to Lithgow's Ltd, reflecting the change of ownership nearly thirty years earlier. It is perhaps unfair to describe the firm as the Henry Ford of Clyde shipbuilding and their products as the maritime equivalent of the Model T. However, they did build large numbers of simple, economical cargo boats rather than high-class liners or naval vessels. In 1890 they turned out twenty-six sailing ships plus hulls for eight steamers. They brought a degree of standardization to shipbuilding which was probably unique for the time, producing about fifty large sailing ships of the same hull shape. In the mid 1890s, by which time even the most cost-effective sailing ship was becoming uncompetitive by comparison with triple-expansion engined steamships, they began to build tramp steamers of standard design. Unglamorous their policy may have been but the firm was more profitable than most shipbuilders and was better able cope with the ups and downs of the demand for ships.

In the nineteenth century the Clyde became by far the most important shipbuilding river in Scotland but this did not mean that east-coast shipbuilding was insignificant. With the transition from wood and sail to iron and steam most of the numerous small yards disappeared and the tendency was for the industry to become concentrated in a few centres.

In Aberdeen, as in other east-coast ports at the end of the eighteenth century, there was a well-established shipbuilding industry turning out vessels for the coasting trade and other small craft. By the middle of the nineteenth century, however, Aberdeen firms had gained a unique reputation as builders of fast ocean-going sailing vessels, and in particular the clipper ships for the China tea trade, and other trades involving high-value cargoes. The goods which reached the market first obtained the best prices and there was therefore pressure on the shipowners to have the fastest vessels in the trade. The clippers owed much of their speed to a redesigned underwater shape and in particular to a much sharper bow than had been usual. This was first seen on the *Scottish Maid*, of 142 tons, built by Alexander Hall in 1839. Although small, it attracted much attention and influenced the design of subsequent ships, both in Aberdeen and on the Clyde. Hall's went on to built many fine clippers, in addition to ships of other types. There were another two firms in Aberdeen particularly noted for their clipper ships. Walter Hood & Company were builders of the well-known and long-lived rival to the *Cutty Sark*, the *Thermopylae* completed in 1868. The firm of Duthie's combined shipowning and shipbuilding. It was founded in 1815 by William Duthie, a ship-owner with strong interests in the Australian trade. An Aberdeen firm which started as engineers and then moved into iron shipbuilding was Hall, Russell & Company. The firm was established in 1864 and built their first ship in 1868. Two of the founding partners, James and William Hall, were connected with the old-established firm of Alexander Hall & Company, which dated back to 1790.

In Dundee the sizeable wooden shipbuilding industry had withered away by about 1870. As in the west, the changes from

Although the world-famous tea clipper, Cutty Sark, *was built on the Clyde, the most important centre for the building of these fast sailing ships was Aberdeen. This is the* Cutty Sark's *great rival,* Thermopylae, *built by Walter Hood in 1868.*

wood to iron and sail to steam were led by the engineers, rather than by traditional shipbuilders. A few early examples of iron ships were built on the Tay by engineering firms but the major Dundee iron shipbuilders, Gourlay Brothers and the Caledon Shipbuilding Company did not appear on the scene until sometime later. The origin of Gourlay Brothers goes back to the Dundee Foundry, started around 1790. The Foundry received its first order for a marine engine in 1829. In 1846 the Gourlays took over and they began iron shipbuilding in 1854. In the twenty-year period 1881-1900 Gourlay's turned out almost half of all shipping built in Dundee. The other big shipyard, the Caledon, developed out of the Tay Foundry, started in 1866 by W B Thompson to supply industrial steam engines and other equipment. Shipbuilding began in 1874, with the ships' machinery coming from the Tay Foundry, which continued to build factory steam engines alongside the marine engines. In the 1880s the firm had a shipyard on the Clyde at Whiteinch, but this was a short-lived venture, closing before the end of the decade. The company became the Caledon Shipbuilding & Engineering Company in 1896. In 1914, by which time Gourlay's had closed down, it was the largest shipbuilding company in the east of Scotland.

On the Forth, the story was much the same, with the steady decline of the numerous small yards building wooden vessels mainly for local owners. A long-lived Leith firm was that of Robert Menzies & Son who began in 1793 and survived, latterly as ship repairers, into the 1960s. Their most famous ship was the wooden paddle steamer *Sirius*, which was fitted with engines by the Clyde firm of Thomas Wingate & Company. Built in 1837 for operation between London and Cork, this modest-sized ship was chartered for two transatlantic voyages in 1838 and became the first vessel to make the crossing solely by steam power. An important nineteenth-century Leith shipbuilder started in 1846 as an offshoot of the Newcastle firm, R & W Hawthorn, which supplied many locomotives to the early Scottish railway companies. Initially the Leith works assembled parts brought from Newcastle by sea but later complete locomotives were built. In 1850 a separate firm, Hawthorn & Company, took over. This continued to build locomotives but also expanded into marine engineering and then shipbuilding at both Granton and Leith. Another significant Leith firm in the nineteenth century was Ramage & Ferguson, which was established in 1877 by two ship-builders who had been employed by firms on the Clyde. Ramage came from William Denny & Brothers and Ferguson from Barclay, Curle & Company, Glasgow. Their output was varied and included large sailing ships and luxurious steam yachts.

In the Kirkcaldy area there were yards building wooden vessels at Burntisland, Dysart, Buckhaven, Methil and West Wemyss, as well as Kirkcaldy itself, but these gradually disappeared. Iron and steam came to the area through the efforts of John Key who established an engineering business in Kirkcaldy in 1850, and then set up the Abden shipyard, Kinghorn, in 1864.

Building a wooden sailing ship at Dysart, on the Forth, c1880.
The frames have been erected and the planking is being fixed.

The first yard at Grangemouth was set up by J Cowie in 1786. About ten years later it was being operated by Alexander Hart, who built William Symington's first steamboat which was tested on the Forth & Clyde Canal in 1801. Thomas Adamson, who had interests in shipyards in Dundee and Alloa, took over the yard in 1825 and reorganized it so that larger vessels could be built. Under yet another operator, the firm of Dobson & Charles, the yard was re-equipped after 1878 to enable iron ships to be built. This firm failed in 1884 and the site was then sold to new company, the Grangemouth Dockyard Company. They prospered, and expanded, at different times using yards at Greenock and Alloa, in addition to Grangemouth. The firm was to remain in business at Grangemouth for over a hundred years.

At Kincardine two very early wooden paddle steamers fitted with Glasgow-made engines, the *Lady of the Lake* and *Morning Star*, were built about 1815 for service on the Forth. Further up river, at Alloa, a late eighteenth century account said that shipbuilding had been 'long and successfully prosecuted here'. About fifty men were then employed in the industry. Two shipyards were intermittently active for most of the nineteenth century, both changing hands frequently. Then in the early 1880s a new firm, Thomson's, set up the Kelliebank yard in which they built both steam and sailing ships. They failed within a few years and the yard was operated by a succession of firms, first the Grangemouth Dockyard Company and then several small firms who each built only a very few ships. Shipbuilding was a precarious business for small firms!

It was not unusual for firms to move from one shipyard site to another in the same district. They may have wanted to expand the scale of the business or the size of the ships required by their customers may have increased beyond the capacity of the site. On occasion, too, shipbuilders had to move because their yard was required for dock developments. However, what was unusual was a complete uprooting and move from one district to another. The Stephen family must hold some sort of record for such moves. They started shipbuilding at Burghead on the Moray Firth sometime around 1750 and had yards at Aberdeen, Arbroath, Dundee and finally settled on the Clyde in 1851 as Alexander Stephen & Sons. However there were considerable overlaps, with various members of the family being involved in different sites. They were in Dundee, for example from 1842 to 1893. In the early days they built mainly small sailing coasters. In Dundee they built up a reputation for whaling ships. On the Clyde they built high-class passenger liners and passenger cargo ships other than those of the largest size, along with a significant number of naval vessels.

An even further travelled firm was Yarrow & Company. They originally began on the Thames in 1865 making a fairly wide range of engineering products but they came to specialize in steam launches. This led in the 1870s to the building of torpedo boats and then torpedo boat 'catchers' or 'destroyers'. Yarrow's became one of the leading firms in the development of these high-speed craft. By the early years of the twentieth century, while the firm was prosperous, the Thames as a shipbuilding river was in terminal decline. Costs were high and skilled labour was increasingly difficult to find. The decision was therefore made to move and after considering a number of locations, a green-field site on the Clyde, at Scotstoun, was selected and by 1908 the new yard was fully operational.

Until about 1860, most shipyards could build almost any type of ship required. However, as the maximum size grew, fewer and fewer yards could build the larger ships. Even with major reconstruction of the older yards the restrictions of the site could not always be overcome. The decision had to be made whether to make the move to a new site further down river, or restrict operations to the smaller ships.

Size was also a consideration in warship building as not every yard had space to build battleships and large cruisers. A further limitation was that the technical standards required were high and not every firm could reach them. The ships were usually designed by Admiralty staff and the construction closely supervised by Admiralty overseers. The dual standards of workmanship required when building both merchant ships and naval vessels in the same yard could cause difficulties. However, for firms such as J & G Thomson and Fairfield, which had invested heavily in the equipment needed to build large liners, the addition of naval work was very desirable. The smaller warships were built by a somewhat wider range of firms but the only real specialist in Scotland was Yarrow & Company.

Russell & Company specialized in cargo vessels of standard design in order to gain the benefits of significant savings in cost. Virtually every other shipbuilder built ships to meet the specific needs of each customer and rarely built two the same. The restrictions which geography placed on some shipbuilders meant that only the smaller types of ship could be produced. The River Cart, for example, became world-famous for the building of dredgers with three firms involved, William Simons & Company and Lobnitz & Company at Renfrew, and Fleming & Ferguson of Paisley. A town which, at first sight, would not be associated with the building of any kind of vessel is Kirkintilloch. However, it is on the Forth & Clyde Canal and many small coasters, known in Scotland as 'puffers', were built there. Because of the restricted width of the canal they had to be launched sideways.

Some types of ship posed particular technical problems and their construction was restricted to one or two firms. Because cross-channel passenger services were usually very competitive, high speed was essential and the ships needed very light, high-powered machinery. The Fairfield yard and William Denny & Brothers were the main Scottish builders in this field. After 1883, when their ship-model experiment tank came into use, Denny's had the competitive edge.

William Denny & Brothers' ship model experiment tank at Dumbarton, which was brought into use in 1883. The illustration shows the rail-mounted carriage used to tow the model being tested. Other models can be seen stored alongside the tank.

Denny's also specialized in shallow-draught river boats, many of them for operation in Burma by the Irrawaddy Flotilla Company, in which they had a financial interest. These were sent out in pieces from Dumbarton and assembled at the Flotilla Company's dockyard near Rangoon. There were other firms building vessels of this kind, including some who were on completely landlocked sites. One such was Alley & McLellan, of Polmadie, Glasgow, a firm of general engineers who built a wide range of products in addition to several hundred ships which were supplied in kit form.

British shipbuilding continued to grow throughout the nineteenth century and into the early years of the twentieth. The Clyde was the most important shipbuilding area in the country, producing about one third of the total British output in the period 1870-1914. At the turn of the century the annual output from the Clyde was in the region of 400,000 tons and in 1913 it reached 750,000 tons, a figure which was never exceeded. From 1900-13 British production amounted to sixty per cent of the world total. However, in the early 1890s the British share had been even higher, at about eighty per cent of a smaller total. Foreign competition first became apparent in the mid 1890s. The newly arrived competitors, principally Germany and the United States, had new and better equipped yards than the British shipbuilders but, even so, they could not at first compete on price without subsidies.

The early years of the twentieth century saw the introduction of major new technical developments in propulsion, in the steam turbine and the diesel engine. The turbine was pioneered in Britain, the Denny-built Clyde steamer *King Edward* of 1901 being the world's first turbine-powered merchant ship. There was a widespread feeling that it would replace the reciprocating steam engine more or less completely. However, experience soon showed that the turbine was only economically worthwhile in applications where very high power was required, such as warships and sizeable passenger ships, or where the maximum power had to be installed in a restricted space. It was the diesel engine, initially limited to a modest power output, which proved to be capable of development in power and efficiency to the point where it is now the usual method of powering ships of all types, except in very special circumstances. Originally invented in Germany by Dr Rudolph Diesel, the main development work on the engine took place on the Continent. The first large sea-going diesel-engined ship was the *Selandia*, built in Denmark in 1912. Many British firms acquired licenses to manufacture Continental marine-engine designs but the British involvement in the development of new and improved designs was relatively small, and the Scottish contribution insignificant.

2 Two World Wars and their Aftermath

Although the industry prospered in the years before the outbreak of World War I, and the war itself placed unprecedented demands on the shipyards, there was serious trouble ahead. As the end of the war approached there was an air of confidence among both shipbuilders and shipowners. On the Forth, at Burntisland, a completely new shipyard was created by the brothers Wilfred and Amos Ayre, from Tyneside, who had wide experience of the industry. The keel of the first ship was laid in June 1918. At Leith, Henry Robb, the shipyard manager of Ramage & Ferguson, established his own firm in 1917. He took six men with him from Ramage & Ferguson, leased a workshop and initially did repairs only. His first ship, built in 1923, was a dredger for India. In 1924 and 1926 Robb took over nearby shipyards belonging to companies in liquidation and then in 1935 he acquired the yard of his former employer, Ramage & Ferguson. Up river at Alloa one of the shipyards attracted the attention of London financiers led by Basil Zaharoff, one of the principal salesmen for the English shipbuilding and armaments firm of Vickers. The yard was acquired in 1916 and renamed by the new owners the Forth Shipbuilding & Engineering Company. On the Clyde, a new company, the Blythswood Shipbuilding Company was established at Scotstoun, Glasgow, in 1919 as a specialist builder of the then new oil tankers. In addition many of the leading Clyde firms, including Fairfield, William Beardmore and Alexander Stephen invested considerable sums of money in extending and re-equipping their yards.

Submarine E35 being built at the Clydebank yard of John Brown & Company, Clydebank, in 1916. The submarine was one of the new weapons first used on a large scale during World War I.

Because of the great demand for ships to replace wartime losses, second-hand vessels fetched very high prices in the immediate post-war period. Some shipowners decided that this was the time to sell out and do other things with their substantial gains. There had always been financial links between builders and owners, usually with the builders being involved in shipowning. Now, the investment was largely in the other direction as shipowners acquired shipbuilders in an effort to ensure that they could have ships quickly and at favourable prices. This activity was all based on the false premise that the boom conditions would last. They did not, and by 1922 the house of cards had collapsed. Not all shipbuilders had believed in the never-ending boom. The brothers Henry and Sir James Lithgow of Lithgows Ltd were convinced, unlike almost everybody else, that there was a serious and chronic excess of shipbuilding capacity in Britain and they were not tempted into any major expansion projects. With substantial cash reserves they were able to survive, even though orders were scarce.

Some of the firms set up during the boom conditions of the war and the immediate postwar years proved better able to weather the subsequent slump than many old-established firms. The Burntisland Shipbuilding Company, by good management, tight financial control and, like Lithgows, a considerable degree of standardization in the ships they built, was able to obtain a share of the few orders available. On the face of it Henry Robb's expansion of facilities by the acquisition of the yards of neighbouring firms in liquidation might have appeared over-ambitious in the depressed interwar years, but like Burntisland they were able to obtain a share of the available orders. Seventy-six ships totalling 40,049 gross tons were built in the years 1925-38. On the Clyde, the Blythswood Shipbuilding Company also survived and prospered, having anticipated correctly that tankers would be a growth area of the market. One of the casualties was Zaharoff's Forth Shipbuilding & Engineering Company at Alloa, which closed around 1923.

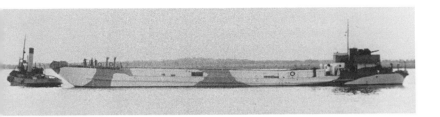

One of the many tank landing craft built during World War II at Alloa, on the Forth, by structural engineering firms, rather than shipbuilders.

As the depression continued there was a growing recognition that excess capacity was a major problem, and one which would not go away without some action. National Shipbuilders Security Ltd was established in 1930 with the aim of buying disused or under-used yards, and ensuring that they were taken out of ship-building. It was hoped that the resulting reduction in capacity would lessen the ruinous competition for the orders which were available. James Lithgow was one of the leading instigators of this scheme and most shipbuilders became involved. It was funded by shares taken up by the participating builders plus a levy of one per cent of the value of tonnage launched. In addition it had government blessing and received a loan from the Bank of England. Eleven Scottish shipyards, all in the west, were partly or wholly closed between 1931 and 1937. It is ironical that among the yards closed was one of the most modern in the country, created primarily for warship building, by William Beardmore & Company on a green-field site at Dalmuir in 1905. National Shipbuilders Security did not provide anything like a complete answer to the problems of the industry but drastic action was essential and it may be that what was done was too little and too late. Prosperity was restored to shipbuilding only by the approach of another war.

During World War II existing shipyards were once again working to capacity on both new building and repairs. Firms with little or no previous experience of shipbuilding also became involved in the industry. The process of building a steel ship has similarities to the building of anything else in steel and it is not surprising, therefore, that firms used to building bridges, storage tanks and other such structural steelwork found themselves required to build ships. For example, 157 tank landing craft were built at Alloa by two firms of structural engineers, Arrol and the Motherwell Bridge & Engineering Company.

The boom which followed this war was perhaps less frenetic than that after 1918 and it lasted somewhat longer. Throughout the 1950s demand was buoyant as wartime losses were replaced. Passenger ships, one of the main products of many Clyde yards, formed a large part of the output in this period. However, the first jet airliners came into service on the North Atlantic in 1958. The increase in speed and reduced cost of air travel resulted in fewer passengers travelling by sea and the demand for passenger vessels declined rapidly. Other markets also shrank, especially where they had been dependent on close links which no longer existed between shipyard and customer. The worldwide demand was rising but much of this was for very large oil tankers and bulk carriers which Scottish yards had not the space to build. After the boom the British shipbuilding industry was exposed to the full blast of competition from European shipyards which had been steadily modernizing, especially those in Scandinavia, and in Germany where in effect new shipyards had been created on the sites of old yards destroyed during the war. There was, too, competition on the way from Japan and later Korea.

Little had been invested in British shipyards between the wars because of the depressed trading conditions. During World War II the existing equipment was simply worked harder and in the boom conditions of the immediate postwar period modernization would have caused too much disruption. As long as the order books were full few people in the industry appear to have given much thought to the future. Several yards spent considerable sums on modernization in the early 1960s but by then it was too late. Orders were drying up and the costs involved in re-equipment were not being recovered. In 1963 William Denny & Brothers announced that they were going into voluntary liquidation. Two years later Fairfield's were forced to call in the receiver, at a time when they had orders worth £32 million and had just completed a modernization programme. A package was put together with government help to try to save the yard and in December 1965 Fairfields (Glasgow) Ltd was set up. This was essentially an experiment to see whether, with a new and more open style of shipyard management, the long-standing problems of bad labour relations and endless demarcation disputes could be overcome. Coupled with better training, this would make possible the introduction of the modern production techniques being used elsewhere in the

The fisheries research vessel Scotia *built by at Ferguson Shipbuilders, Port Glasgow, for the Scottish Office Agriculture Environment and Fisheries Department. This complex ship, fitted with the latest scientific equipment, was handed over early in 1998.*

engineering industry and, it was hoped, result in a shipyard able to survive the international competition.

By this time it was apparent that not just the Clyde but the whole of British shipbuilding was in serious trouble. In February 1965 the Labour government had set up an inquiry chaired by R M Geddes and this reported in 1966. Amalgamation was offered as the remedy and from this recommendation came the formation of Upper Clyde Shipbuilders, incorporating John Brown, Charles Connell, Fairfield, Alexander Stephen and Yarrow, and the amalgamation of the lower Clyde firms of Scott and Lithgow, as Scott Lithgow Ltd. Upper Clyde Shipbuilders had a short and unhappy existence, and went into receivership in 1971. Yarrow's had already managed to extract themselves from the company. After the famous 'work-in' at Clydebank, the John Brown yard went to the American oil-rig builder Marathon, and Fairfield and Connell were reformed as Govan Shipbuilders Ltd. The saga of UCS hit the headlines and overshadowed what was happening elsewhere. It was easily forgotten that things were, for a time, rather better in other areas. On the lower Clyde at Scott Lithgow, and with the east-coast shipbuilders, there was none of the trauma which afflicted the yards on the upper reaches of the Clyde.

Unfortunately, the 1970s saw a huge increase in the price of oil and a major slump in orders for new ships. By 1976 the industry was in a worse state than before, with the misery spreading to firms which had until then been reasonably prosperous. In an effort to salvage something, the Labour government nationalized the industry in 1977 and made financial assistance available. Two years later a Conservative government was elected under Margaret Thatcher and privatization was the order of the day. The treatment given to the admittedly ailing shipbuilding industry was rather like the action of a gardener who pulls up a sickly plant by the roots periodically to find out why it is not doing well. The result in both cases is likely to be death!

By the end of the 1980s there was little left of the Scottish shipbuilding industry. Scott Lithgow on the lower Clyde and, on the

The up-to-date shipyard of Ferguson Shipbuilders, Port Glasgow, showing ships on the building berths and the extensive prefabrication sheds. Next door to this modernized shipyard is the ancient Newark Castle, which is in the care of Historic Scotland.

east coast, Robb-Caledon (Leith and Dundee) and Hall, Russell (Aberdeen) had all closed. At the time of writing there are, apart from a few builders of fishing vessels and other small craft, only three yards left. The warship specialist Yarrow Shipbuilders continues at Scotstoun. The Fairfield yard of Govan Shipbuilders has been Norwegian owned since 1988, as Kvaerner Govan, and at Port Glasgow there is the small yard of Ferguson Shipbuilders.

3 Owners, Managers and Workers

There is little information available about those engaged in ship-building in early times. However, by the time the *Great Michael* was being built in the early sixteenth century the shipwright would have emerged as a specialized tradesman. Because this was a vessel of exceptional size, even the resources of the royal dockyard would be overstretched and 'all wrights of Scotland, yea, and many other strangers, were at her device, by the king's commandment'. All available shipwrights, supplemented by other tradesmen, from Scotland and elsewhere were drawn into the building of one of the biggest ships of her time.

From small and scattered beginnings, shipbuilding grew into a major source of employment in Scotland. By middle of the nineteenth century there were 18,000 people working in the industry and the number had trebled by 1911. In addition there were many more working in industries which depended directly on shipbuilding.

It was the development of the steamship which resulted in the explosive growth of shipbuilding in Scotland. Most of the leaders of this revolution came from the same sort of background. They were millwrights and blacksmiths, versatile workers in timber, iron and masonry as required, able to build and repair machinery for grain milling and other purposes. Henry Bell came from just such a background. He was born on 7 April 1767, the fifth son of Patrick Bell, millwright and miller at Torphichen Mill in what was then called Linlithgowshire but later became West Lothian. Young Henry received his early education at the parish school in Torphichen but at the age of nine he was sent to lodge with an uncle and aunt in Falkirk so that he could attend the burgh school, because the master there had a high reputation as a teacher of mathematics. Unfortunately, by the time his formal education finished at the age of thirteen, his writing, spelling and grammar were still poor and this was something he was to regret in later life. Then in 1780 Bell went to learn the work of a stonemason with one of his relatives. After three years he was apprenticed to an uncle who, like his father, was a millwright. His apprenticeship finished in 1786 and the next few years show that here was no ordinary nineteen-year-old just out of his time. Instead of settling down as a country millwright, which would not have been difficult with his family connections, he set about broadening his knowledge and experience. First he spent a year with the Bo'ness shipbuilders, Shaw & Hart, so that he could learn 'ship-modelling'. By this was meant the design of ships, and particularly the form of the hull. Then he went for a year to the mining district of Lanarkshire, to work for the Bellshill-based engineer James Inglis. In 1788 Bell moved to London, to work for a period of eighteen months with one of the greatest of the millwrights and engineers of the day, John Rennie, a fellow Scot. Rennie came from East Lothian and had moved to London in 1854. As a consulting engineer he built up an extensive practice and was involved in a wide range of projects including canals, bridges, harbours and a large steam-driven flour mill in London. This last job was under construction while Bell was with Rennie. By the time Henry Bell returned to Scotland around 1790 he had experience of shipbuilding and of steam-powered machinery. It is very likely that he was beginning to think about the use of steam to power a boat, although it was to be over twenty years before he was able to have the *Comet* built. Meanwhile he had to earn a living and he therefore started as a builder and carpenter in Glasgow. By 1794 he was also describing himself as an architect. In 1806-7 he built the Baths Inn at Helensburgh which he and his wife then ran.

As the industry developed from the pioneering stage, this involvement of the engineers continued. Around thirty-eight marine engines were built in Glasgow before 1820, by eight firms. In 1825, when James Cleland recorded that there were sixty-eight engines in steamboats, he also noted that there were 242 engines working on land in the Glasgow district. This gives some indication of just how widespread was the practical experience of building and operating steam engines. Marine engines posed their own special problems but the pioneers had a sound base for their step into this new field.

The men who established the Clyde shipbuilding industry on a firm foundation were the cousins David and Robert Napier. Both were born in Dumbarton, David in 1790 and Robert in the following year. Their fathers, John and James, worked as blacksmiths in the town, until John left in 1802 to set up his own business in Glasgow. David was trained by him and by 1810, at the age of twenty, he was effectively running the business. Having built the boiler for Henry Bell's *Comet* and followed the subsequent progress of steam navigation, David Napier decided to become more involved. As he later wrote 'Seeing steam navigation was likely to succeed, I erected new works in Camlachie', on the east side of Glasgow. This was in 1814-15. There he made his first marine engine for a vessel called the *Marion*, which he had built for

Robert Napier (1791-1876) was the leading light in Clyde marine engineering and steamship building in the formative years of the industry.

him at Dumbarton in 1816 by Archibald MacLachlan. This vessel represented not only Napier's first venture into marine engineering, it was also the first of many forays into ship-owning. He ran the *Marion* on the Clyde for a year and then moved it to Loch Lomond where it provided the first steamer service. After building engines for some forty ships in Glasgow he decided in 1836 to move to London. He set up an iron ship-building firm at Millwall but this did not prosper. Nevertheless, he was still full of ideas and patented several important innovations relating to marine engineers and boilers.

William Denny (1847-1887) was the third member of the renowned family of Dumbarton shipbuilder to bear the name. His early death was a great loss to the family firm of William Denny & Brothers.

Robert Napier began his working life by serving a formal apprenticeship with his father. After spells working as an employee in Edinburgh and then Glasgow, in 1815 he bought a black-smith's business in the latter city. He began making equipment for the local textile and other manufacturing industries and about 1821 built his first steam engine, for a flax spinning mill in Dundee. The first marine engine followed in 1823 for a wooden paddle steamer called the *Leven*, built at Dumbarton by the first William Denny. Robert Napier was to become the most influential marine engineer and shipbuilder of his time but by the early 1860s change was in the air. The firm which he founded was largely run by Napier himself and his long-serving manager David Elder. As often happens, with advancing years they became resistant to change. Two of Napier's sons had been taken into partnership in 1853 but this did not work out and Robert Napier had to continue the active management of the firm, when he would much rather have devoted time to his country house at West Shandon (later to become the Shandon Hydro) and to his art collection. The succession problem was never solved and this led to the demise of the firm in its original form following the death of Robert Napier in 1876.

David Elder was yet another example of a man who came to marine engineering after training as a millwright. He was born in 1785 near Kinross, son of a millwright. After little in the way of formal education, partly because his father had no high opinion of book learning, he started to learn the millwright's trade. By 1804 he was engaged on building work in Edinburgh's new town. Then, like so many of his contemporaries, he went west and by 1814 he was involved in the erection of cotton-spinning mills in Glasgow. He began working for Napier in 1821 and stayed with him until a few years before he (Elder) died in 1866. Perhaps surprisingly David Elder never became a partner in Robert Napier's firm. It may be that he did not want a partnership, preferring to remain a valued and well-rewarded employee. How well rewarded is shown by the terms of a new seven-year agreement made with Napier in 1835. Under this, he was to be paid £250 per annum, plus 7/6d (37.5p) for each Nominal Horse Power of the engines built by the firm. This could amount to a large sum, as exemplified by just one of many contracts in the period of the agreement. Engines were built for the four ships with which Cunard began his transatlantic service in 1840. Each engine was of 420 NHP , a total of 1680 NHP for the four, and therefore worth £630 to David Elder, in addition to his salary. It should be noted that the Nominal Horse Power, or NHP, was a calculated figure based on the dimensions of the engine cylinders and an assumed figure for the steam pressure. In the early days of marine engineering it was a reasonable approximation but as engines were improved the actual power became much greater than the NHP. Nevertheless it remained in use for many years because it indicated physical size of an engine and the amount of work involved in construction. The NHP was therefore an appropriate basis for agreements such as that between Robert Napier and David Elder.

Many men who were trained at Napier's and elsewhere on the Clyde made a point of broadening their experience by working in other parts of the country, and sometimes in other industries, before returning to take up major roles in existing firms or establishing their own shipyards. This second generation of engineers and shipbuilders made an immense contribution to the continuing expansion of the industry in the second half of the nineteenth century. Some left Scotland for good and left their mark elsewhere. Movement of outsiders into the shipbuilding industry in Scotland was less common, but some of those who did come had great influence on the industry.

Alexander C Kirk (1830-1892), pioneer of the triple-expansion engine and one of the most important of the second generation of Clyde marine engineers.

The career of A C Kirk, a son of the manse, born at Barry, near Dundee, about 1830, was more varied than most. On finishing his apprenticeship at Napier's he moved to London where he worked in the drawing office of Maudslay, Sons & Field, a well-known marine engineering firm at that time. When he returned to Scotland it was not to marine engineering but to the shale-oil industry, where he designed plant for processing the oil-bearing shale and the subsequent refining of the oil. His opportunity to return to marine engineering came when John Elder died in 1869. His firm, Randolph, Elder & Company, was reorganized under a new partnership and with the name changed to John Elder & Company. Kirk went to work for the new firm as manager of the engine works and it was while there that he developed the triple-expansion engine with which his name will always be linked.

Walter Brock was another engineer who moved to London, and out of marine engineering, after leaving Napier's. In 1859, after seven years at Napier's, he became head draughtsman with James Simpson & Company of Pimlico, London, who specialized in steam pumping machinery for water-supply systems. Brock returned to Scotland in 1864, initially to his old employer. Then in 1871 he became managing partner at Denny & Company, the engine-building company associated with the Dumbarton shipbuilders, William Denny & Brothers. Technical ability on its own was rarely sufficient to gain a partnership in the family-owned shipbuilding concerns which dominated the industry in the nineteenth century although, as his subsequent work showed, Walter Brock was a very able engineer. A family connection was also necessary and Brock was a nephew of Peter Denny, the leading light in both Denny firms at that time. He spent the rest of his life with the firm, becoming a partner in William Denny & Brothers, as well as Denny & Company, and was active in the firms until two months before his death at the age of seventy-one in 1907. His obituary noted that he had no interests outside his work. This was quite unusual. Despite the pressures of business most engineers and shipbuilders of his generation found time to take some part in the activities of the various technical institutions and perhaps in civic affairs.

One of the few men who did achieve a partnership without family connections, and ultimately became sole partner in a major firm, was William Pearce. Born in Kent in 1833, he was trained at Chatham Dockyard. He initially came to the Clyde in 1863 as a surveyor, inspecting vessels for Lloyds' Register of Shipping, but in the following year he went to Robert Napier & Sons as shipyard manager. Like A C Kirk, Pearce found his opportunity with the reorganization of Randolph, Elder & Company following the death of John Elder. He was offered a partnership in the new firm, becoming one of the three partners in John Elder & Company. In addition to his undoubted abilities as a naval architect and shipbuilder Pearce had a great flair for publicity. It is said that he was responsible for the creation of the 'Blue Riband' held by the liner holding the record for the fastest transatlantic crossing. Certainly

John Elder & Company (the Fairfield Shipbuilding and Engineering Company from 1886) built many record-breakers for the leading shipping firms, and virtually replaced Napier's as the main builder for Cunard. Knowing the ways of the Admiralty from his experience at Chatham Dockyard, Pearce was also able to guide the firm into naval shipbuilding. Under his control it became the leading yard on the Clyde. Pearce was involved in many things outside shipbuilding. He became MP for Govan in 1885 and served on a number of Royal Commissions dealing with nautical matters. It would seem that his frenetic life was more than his body could stand for he died in 1888 aged only fifty-three.

In an industry dominated by family firms, William Pearce (1835-1888) was unusual in being an outsider. Born in Kent and trained at Chatham Dockyard, he became sole partner in one of the leading Clyde firms, the Fairfield Shipbuilding & Engineering Company.

Of those who left Scotland and pursued the rest of their career elsewhere, one of the most interesting is John Scott Russell. He was born in Glasgow in 1808 and, according to some accounts, by the time he was sixteen or seventeen he had graduated from the University. For a time in the 1830s he was manager of a shipyard at Greenock and then in 1844 he moved to London. As one of the most profound thinkers about the problems of ship hydro-dynamics and also the structural design of iron ships, it is not surprising that he became involved with Isambard Kingdom Brunel, and the monster ship *Great Eastern*. This was built between 1854 and 1857 at Scott Russell's shipyard at Millwall, on the site of the yard established by David Napier following his move to London. The *Great Eastern*, after earlier unsuccessful attempts, was eventually launched on 31 January 1858.

As the reputation of the Scottish shipbuilding industry grew, men with experience were called on to help in the setting up and running of shipyards elsewhere. For example, giving evidence in 1886 to a Royal Commission on the Depression in Trade, J Scott of Greenock said that he had set up and managed a shipyard in France for a number of years. Skilled men from the Clyde were often to be found in new yards established in Denmark, Germany and Russia. One of the concerns of the Commission was the effect of foreign competition on British shipyards. Nearer home, the new town of Barrow-in-Furness, Lancashire, was planned and built as a port, steelworks and shipyard. The Barrow Shipbuilding Company was conceived in 1869 as part of this development and its brand new shipyard was planned by the Greenock shipbuilder Robert Duncan. The technical staff and skilled men came from the Clyde and the unskilled labour from Ireland. The yard was well laid out and allowed for successive expansions without the need to change the basic plan. When iron shipbuilding developed in Northern Ireland many of the skilled men came from the Clyde although again the unskilled labour was mostly local.

When the new engineering and iron shipbuilding firms were first established on the Clyde new skills had to be learned. The first marine engineering firms could draw on the experience of the builders of factory steam engines, although it was sometimes felt that their skills were inadequate for the more severe conditions encountered by marine engines. Factory steam engines were bolted to substantial masonry foundations whereas marine engines were supported only by the hull of the ship, and especially in wooden ships this was fairly flexible. The engines themselves had therefore to be more rigidly built so that they were less dependent on the hull for strength. When A C Kirk first went to see Robert Napier's manager, David Elder, about an apprenticeship, he was told to go and work as a joiner for two years. Elder had very firm opinions on the need for rigidity in the frames of marine engines and he felt that house joiners and cartwrights had a greater appreciation of the need for well-fitting joints than the older millwrights who were working for him. Marine engines had many large castings for the cylinders and other parts, and joiners could make the wooden patterns required for use in the foundry. At least one Glasgow engineering firm employed stonemasons because they were used to dressing stones by hammer and chisel to produce flat surfaces. They could learn to do the same with cast iron.

In building iron ships the shaping of frames and plates was blacksmiths' and boilermakers' work, on a large scale. When shipbuilding in iron was developing the shipwrights used to working in wood were reluctant to have anything to do with the new material and their role effectively became limited to preparation of the building berth, erection of the frames and the arrangements for the launch. This division sowed the seeds for some of the demarcation disputes between the trades unions in later

Hydraulic press at the Greenock yard of the Greenock & Grangemouth Dockyard Company about 1905. This was used to shape plates to make them fit the frames of the ship.

years. Curiously, this attitude seems to have been confined to the private shipyards. In the naval dockyards, which at that time built ships as well as repairing them, the shipwrights did the work, whether the ships were of iron or wood, and the boilermakers built and repaired only boilers.

Shipyard workers, particularly riveters and platers, were well-paid by the standards of the time. However, shipbuilding was more subject to fluctuations in trade than most industries, and lay-offs were frequent. A less well-paid job with for example, Glasgow Corporation Tramways or one of the railway companies, offered as compensation a level of job security rare at that time and one that shipyard workers could never hope for. From the shipyard employers' point of view, the ease with which the size of the labour force could be adjusted to meet the needs of the moment acted as a disincentive to the installation of labour-saving machinery. In purely economic terms there was some short-term justification for this way of thinking, although the social consequences were horrendous. The long-term result, however, was old-fashioned and badly equipped yards which became unable to compete in world markets.

During both World Wars many women worked in shipbuilding. The photograph, taken on 8 April 1946, shows Jean, a welder in a Scotstoun, Glasgow, shipyard. SLA

Shipbuilding was always very much a man's job but towards the end of the nineteenth century women too were beginning to find a place, albeit a limited one. As ships became more complex the working drawings became more detailed, and more people needed access to this information. Tracings of the original drawings were made on translucent paper or starched linen cloth and from these the necessary multiple copies could be made. The practice of employing women to prepare the tracings started at the Glasgow locomotive building firm of Dübs & Company in the 1860s and became general in the west of Scotland shipbuilding and engineering industries. David Pollock, writing in 1884, gives an interesting if somewhat patronizing account of the twenty women employed in the drawing office and the ship-model experiment tank at the Dumbarton shipyard of William Denny & Brothers:

> All the girls are selected by written competitive examination, the subjects of examination being arithmetic, writing to dictation, and block-letter printing.
>
> At first it was intended the girls should simply be trained as tracers, but they displayed such aptitude that to tracing was added the inking-in of finished drawings and the reduction of plans from a greater to a less scale. This they do with a very fair degree of accuracy and neatness. The experienced members of the staff are now employed in making displacement calculations, including plotting the results to scale, centre of buoyancy, and meta-centre calculations; calculations of ships' surface, working up and plotting of speed trial results, stability calculations.

Denny's, who undertook a lot of their own furnishing work on their ships instead of sub-contracting it, also employed a considerable number of women on upholstery work, polishing, stained glass and decorative painting. On the latter Pollock remarks that, 'Under the guidance of a lady artist, the employés in this branch have evinced much aptitude and taste for the work.' Including the tracers and others in the drawing office, the firm was employing a total of eighty to a hundred women.

Much of the unskilled labour came from the thousands of unhappy people driven by hard times from the Scottish

Highlands and Ireland to the expanding urban areas of the west of Scotland. Many at first found employment as handloom weavers, whose numbers continued to increase until the 1840s. By the time iron shipbuilding was becoming well-established, large numbers of handloom weavers were facing unemployment, or employment only on starvation wages, because the work was being done by power-driven looms. Labouring on the construction of the expanding railway system was one alternative source of employment and the shipyards were another.

In the early years of the nineteenth century ship design was very much a matter of rule of thumb. Such textbooks as existed were French and the opinion was held, by some, that the ships of the French navy were better than those of the Royal Navy. The Admiralty was sufficiently concerned to organize a School of Naval Architecture in 1811 at Portsmouth. Although the teaching of naval architecture under Admiralty auspices was intermittent it was nevertheless the only formal teaching available in Britain for many years. Even in the first decade of the twentieth century most naval architects with a scientific training had received it while serving with the Admiralty. It was 1881 before there was a course in naval architecture available in Scotland, at the University of Glasgow. The lectureship which made this possible was endowed by the Institution of Engineers and Shipbuilders in Scotland. Then in 1883 John Elder's widow gifted the sum of £12,500 to the University to enable the lectureship to become a full professorship. In memory of her late husband this was named the John Elder Chair of Naval Architecture. A second full-time course in naval architecture became available in Glasgow from 1909, at the Royal Technical College, now Strathclyde University.

Something which is not generally appreciated is the extent to which shipbuilding and shipowning were linked. From the early stages of their careers David Napier and Robert Napier were shipowners and operators as well as builders of marine engines. As mentioned earlier, the *Marion* for which David Napier built his first marine engines in 1816, was operated by him on the Clyde and on Loch Lomond. Two years later, William Denny built for him the *Rob Roy* which he ran between Greenock and Belfast. In 1822 a Parliamentary Select Committee, set up to enquire into the mail service between England and Ireland, described David Napier as 'enterprising and successful, having established Steam Packets between Glasgow and Belfast, Greenock and Liverpool, Holyhead and Dublin, Dover and Calais'. When Robert Napier supplied the Dundee, Perth & London Shipping Company with its first steamers, the *Dundee* and the *Perth*, in 1834, part of the package was that he would arrange training in steam for the officers who were to take command of the new ships. This he did in steamers already operating services in which he had a financial interest. Robert Napier was involved in financing many shipping companies, among them Samuel Cunard's British & North American Royal Mail Steam Packet Company.

Ships built as a speculation might be operated by the builder if a buyer was not found immediately. The screw steamer *City of Glasgow*, built of iron by Tod & McGregor, was one such. After completion in 1850 the ship made four successful voyages between Greenock and New York, and was then bought by William Inman, for the newly formed Liverpool & Philadelphia Steamship Company. Unfortunately she had a short working life. On 1 March 1854 she set off for America with 480 people on board and disappeared.

When Peter Denny, of William Denny & Brothers, Dumbarton, died in 1895 he had shareholdings in eleven shipping companies. Among them was the Irrawaddy Flotilla Company which was formed in 1876 to operate extensive river services in Burma. Denny's built 250 vessels for the company and the profits on their construction were well above those earned on most other work. Peter Denny often had ships built for him by the firm, as speculations. They might be sold while still on the stocks but if not, they would be operated on Denny's own account, using the well-known Glasgow shipowners, Patrick Henderson & Company (familiarly known as Paddy Henderson's) as agents. Shipowning was not always profitable, however. When the Denny family tried to develop services on the River Plate, in South America, as they had done so successfully on the Irrawaddy, the result was a disaster. La Platense Flotilla Company, set up in 1882, had to be wound up in 1890 with losses of around half a million pounds.

A shipbuilder with many shipping interests, of a somewhat different sort, was W T Lithgow of Russell & Company, Port Glasgow, builders of simple cargo ships, first sailing vessels and then steamers. To keep the yard occupied in times of slack trade Lithgow would often take part payment for a ship in shares. When he died in 1908 he left shares in a total of eighty-one individual ships and shipping companies.

4 Ship Design

As mentioned in the previous chapter, shipbuilders would sometimes start to build ships 'on spec', in order to keep the core of the labour force employed when trade was slack. Generally, however, vessels are built to the specific requirements of a particular customer. The process of designing the ship must therefore start with the customer, who has to consider carefully what kind of ship he needs. Decisions have to be made on matters such as passenger and cargo capacity, speed, type of machinery and other variables which influence commercial viability. In addition, there may be dimensional constraints because of the intended use of particular ports or waterways such as the Panama Canal. The larger shipping companies have their own naval architects who, in collaboration with the commercial staff, will develop the outline of what is needed into a much more detailed specification. A consultant naval architect might be employed to do this if the customer does not have one on the staff. On the basis of the outline requirements or of the full specification a number of builders will be asked to submit a quotation. In the case of a new British warship, the Admiralty has to assess the likely operational needs within the expected life of the vessel. Based on this, the

The drawing office was a vital part of all shipyards. This is one of the smaller shipyards, Cran & Somerville, of Leith, who specialised in tugs. The yard closed in 1926. SLA

ship would normally be designed by the Royal Corps of Naval Constructors, who form part of the Admiralty's own staff. Sometimes, however, shipbuilding firms might be given responsibility for the design work.

The job of the naval architect, working closely with the engineer responsible for the design of the machinery, is to develop the specification into a set of plans sufficiently detailed to make it possible to build a ship which meets all the requirements. In designing a ship a great many factors have to be considered and, like all engineering design, it is combination of science and art: science takes the designer only so far and thereafter it is a creative art. Past experience will suggest likely design solutions. One variable for which a figure, based on experience, has to be assumed at a fairly early stage, is the total weight of the complete ship, ie the structure of the hull, machinery and all fittings and furnishings. The way this weight is divided between the various components depends on what the ship will be used for. For example, high speed was a very important requirement for the transatlantic passenger liners of years gone by. The machinery had to be very powerful and, with its fuel, occupied a lot of space, leaving less for passengers and cargo. The Cunard liners *Lusitania* and *Mauretania*, which went into service in 1907, were built very much with speed as the prime requirement. Intended as armed merchant cruisers in time of war, their construction was heavily subsidized, as was their operation. In return the Admiralty had a very large say in their design. They were of 31,500 tons gross and could carry 2,160 passengers. With a speed of 26 knots, they needed machinery of 72,500 horsepower (54,100 kilowatts) which burned 1,000 tons of coal per day. Without the massive Government subsidy they would never have been built. Cunard's *Aquitania* of 1914 was, like the *Lusitania*, built at Clydebank, but without the special subsidy. It was thus a very different, and much more commercial ship. At 45,647 gross tons and able to carry 3,230 passengers, the new ship was significantly larger than the *Lusitania*. However, because the service speed was just 23 knots, machinery of only 60,000 horse power (44,750 kilowatts) was required, with a substantial saving in coal. The result was a ship with greater earning capacity and lower running costs.

As the design of a ship is worked out in more detail it may become apparent that the initial figure assumed for the weight is wrong. This is then altered and the design revised. It might be necessary to go round this 'design spiral' several times before a satisfactory result is achieved. Once the design has been finalized, the builder has a major problem if the actual weight of the ship when completed turns out to be significantly greater than expected. This means a reduction in carrying capacity and under the terms of contract between the builder and customer there is likely to be a financial penalty. At worst, the ship may be rejected by the customer. 'Paper' ships are easily altered but trying to reduce the weight of a ship after completion is much more difficult!

A great many things have to be considered in the course of the design work. Strength and stability are the first essentials.

Resistance to motion through the water, and hence the power needed for propulsion, must be as small as possible in order to minimize the fuel consumed, because this forms a large part of overall running costs. The development of the ship model test tank has greatly assisted the creation of more efficient hull forms. From the resistance measured by testing scale models of proposed hull designs, the resistance of the full size ship, and thus the power to drive it at the required speed, can be predicted with some confidence. Nowadays in almost all circumstances diesel engines are the automatic choice for propulsion but there are several varieties and the optimum form for a particular application has to be selected. In addition to the main engines, modern ships require a large amount of auxiliary machinery for such things as electricity generation, ventilation and air-conditioning, cargo handling and, for some trades, refrigeration. All this has to be chosen, positions in the ship decided and the associated pipework and electrical systems designed.

A ship is a temporary home for its crew and perhaps a large number of passengers, and therefore has to be made habitable, furnished and decorated. Even in the early days of the steamship there was great emphasis in the design and decoration of the passenger accommodation, at least for the cabin or first class passengers. The *Comet* was well-enough appointed but the best cabin of the *Elizabeth*, which began to operate a competing service in February 1813, was positively palatial, if owner John Thomson is to be believed!

> A sofa, clothed with marone [ie maroon], is placed at one end of the cabin, and gives the whole a warm and cheerful appearance. There are twelve small windows, each furnished with marone curtains with tassels, fringes and velvet cornices, ornamented with gilt ornaments...

He was operating in direct competition with the *Comet* between Glasgow and Greenock. His main advantage was that he had a larger and faster ship, but the quality of the accommodation was

The library on board the Cunard liner Campania, *completed at the Fairfield yard in 1893, showing the ornate finish typical of the first-class accommodation on major passenger liners.*

also regarded as very important. A further feature of the *Elizabeth* was bookshelves, 'containing a selection of the best authors, for the amusement and edification' of the passengers. The seagoing library had been born, and was to become a common amenity on passenger ships. The design of the passenger accommodation remained very important, usually following the fashions of the day but often in more extravagant forms than the shore-based equivalents. Not surprisingly, there is much more information about what was provided for passengers travelling first class, than about the conditions in which the poor emigrants travelled. Steerage accommodation was basic, even spartan, but it did improve over the years.

Perhaps the most basic factor in ship design, and one which has an influence on almost everything else, is the material used in construction. For thousands of years wood was the usual material but by the early years of the nineteenth century suitable timber was becoming scarce. Moreover, the size of ships was increasing and it had become clear that for a wooden ship there was a practical limit to the length of about 300 feet (91 metres). The problem was lack of longitudinal stiffness and the greater the length the more serious this became. It was Robert Seppings, the Master Shipwright at Chatham dockyard in the first decade of the nineteenth century, who first really understood the nature of the problem. By designing the structure with a system of diagonal bracing in the lower part of the hull, the stiffness was significantly increased. This bracing was of timber to begin with but iron was later used. Seppings also made extensive use of forged iron 'knees', the brackets connecting the deck beams to the frame timbers. While this system of construction arose from the need to improve warships, it was also applied to some merchant vessels. The Greenock firm of Scott & Company adopted Seppings' principles at an early stage. Seppings' revolutionary method of construction can be seen by visitors to the frigate *Unicorn*, completed at Chatham dockyard in 1824, and now preserved in Victoria Dock, Dundee.

In the 1860s the use of iron frames with wooden planking became popular. The tea clipper *Cutty Sark*, built at Dumbarton in 1869 by Scott & Linton, is a notable surviving example of this type of composite construction. Some shippers of high value commodities such as tea thought that a long spell in an iron hull might taint the goods. However, there was a more serious problem with iron hulls. Until satisfactory anti-fouling paints were available, iron ships sailing in tropical waters suffered greatly from the build-up of marine growths such as barnacles on the hull, greatly reducing the speed. Wooden ships could have their bottoms protected by nailed-on copper sheet, which discouraged the marine life. The era of composite construction was short-lived and iron soon became the accepted material for almost all vessels.

The iron produced by smelting iron ore in a blast furnace is brittle and therefore not suitable for the hull of a ship because it would crack instead of 'giving' as the hull flexes due to the action of the waves. However, it flows easily when melted and could be used in a foundry to produce castings for many engine components such as cylinders. Iron from the blast furnace contains a significant amount of carbon and it is this which makes it brittle. To make it tough and suitable for shipbuilding it had to undergo a refining process which removed almost all the carbon, leaving wrought iron, or malleable iron as it was called in Scotland. The next development was the replacement of wrought iron by iron containing a small, closely controlled amount of carbon, in other words, steel. It had been known for many years that steel was stronger than wrought iron but it was expensive to produce and only available in small quantities. Although steel was widely used for cutlery and tools requiring a sharp cutting edge, to be of general use in engineering and shipbuilding there had to be cheap ways of making it in large quantities. Such processes were developed in the 1850s and 1860s by Bessemer, Siemens and others but initially there were problems with the quality of the steel produced and shipbuilders were doubtful about its reliability. When the changeover from iron to steel did come, however, it came quickly. The Dumbarton firm of William Denny & Brothers built the first ocean-going steel ship, the *Rotomahana*, in 1879, followed by the much larger *Buenos Ayrean* later in the same year. Three years later Robert Duncan & Company of Greenock became the first firm in Scotland to change totally to steel and within a few years its use was almost universal.

On the face of it, reinforced concrete is an unlikely material from which to build a ship. However, steel shortages during World War I encouraged things which might not have been tried otherwise. From 1917 to 1920, as a result of an initiative by the Ministry of Shipping, the Scottish Concrete Shipbuilding Company was established at Greenock. They built ten vessels, both coasters and dumb barges, ie barges without propelling machinery. Although the initial experiences were satisfactory the idea was not developed further. Glass-fibre-reinforced plastic is now used extensively for small pleasure boats. It can also be used for larger vessels and in recent years Yarrow's have built a number of minesweepers using this material. These had to be of non-magnetic materials as far as possible in minimize the risk from magnetic mines. Although wood still has its uses and materials such as glass-fibre-reinforced plastic have a role, steel is still by far the most commonly used material in shipbuilding. The design of ships will change to meet new requirements, as it always has done, but steel seems likely to remain the basic material for the foreseeable future.

5 Building a Ship

The process of building a ship is a complicated one, with variations in practice from yard to yard. The traditional method was piece-by-piece assembly on an open-air building berth from which the ship would in due course be launched. Construction started with the laying of the keel, which on an iron or steel ship is not the deep blade associated with yachts, but a plate lying flat and running the full length of the ship, along the centre-line of the bottom. Laying the keel was traditionally an occasion for ceremony, and also for payment of part of the contract price, but in fact much work had been done before this stage was reached. The berth had to be prepared and in particular the keel blocks, on which the keel plates were assembled, had to be positioned. They had to be carefully lined up before work started, otherwise the ship would be distorted, and they had to be set at the correct slope so that the ship could be launched.

Before the ship could be assembled the various pieces had to be formed to the required shapes and sizes. In describing the processes involved in the mid-nineteenth century, the eyewitness account written by the journalist David Bremner for *The Scotsman* in 1868 can hardly be bettered, beyond amplifying some parts which he rather glossed over; indeed there were few significant changes until well after the end of World War II:

> The working drawings are passed to the moulders, whose 'loft' is so large that the full-sized outlines of a vessel of 5000 tons may be

drawn on the floor, which is merely a gigantic blackboard. There the drawings are enlarged to the full dimensions in chalk, so that the form of each frame or rib, and the dimensions and curve of each plate, may be ascertained exactly. Adjoining the moulding loft is a workshop, the floor of which is paved with blocks of cast iron, pierced at regular intervals with holes about an inch in diameter. On this floor full-sized outlines of the frames of the vessel are drawn in chalk. With the exception of a few amidships, no two ribs are exactly alike, so that much care and no small amount of skill are required on the part of the workmen in this department. The ribs are formed of angle-iron - that is, iron having a section like a letter L. After the floor has been prepared by placing a series of pegs in the holes bordering on the chalk line, the iron bar intended for the rib is taken out of the furnace in which it has been heating, and, by pressure against the pegs and some hammering, is brought to the required shape with great facility. After the frames and plates have been shaped, they are taken to punching or drilling machines, by which the holes for the rivets are made.

Chalked lines on the floor of the mould loft were always liable to be lost. The practice therefore grew up of cutting or 'scrieving' the lines into the surface of a sort of false floor made of smooth planed boards laid edge to edge. This 'scrieve board', as it was called, gave a permanent record of the shape of the frames which could be kept as long as required. It might be used if another ship with identical lines was to be built. Wooden templates were made from the lines drawn or scrieved in the mould loft and these were used to mark out the lines on the cast-iron blocks which formed the floor of the workshop.

Something omitted by Bremner was the need to adjust the angle of most of the frames so that the plating would fit snugly. The midships frames could be left with right-angled cross-sections, but the others had to be bevelled, ie the angle adjusted to something other than a right angle. Each one was different and the angle also varied along its length. This was a very skilful job, done by hammering the heated frames. In later years use was

The frame-bending shed at the Caledon Shipbuilding & Engineering Company, Dundee, c1935. In the background are the furnaces used to heat the steel for the frames before bending.

made of bevelling machines. After the end of World War II there were changes in the techniques used in the mould loft. The full-size drawing on the floor was replaced by a one-tenth size drawing which was photographed on a glass plate. This could then be projected in the frame-bending shop to give the required full-size shape of the frame. Plating was also rather more complicated that Bremner indicated, especially the cutting and shaping of the plates near the bow and stern of the vessel. Use was made of half-block models, on which the positions of the plates were marked and the shapes worked out. The plates were then cut to shape and bent as necessary. The frames, which defined the shape of the vessel, were erected and then covered by the plates. A multitude of rivets was used to fasten the parts together, until the introduction of welding.

One of the pioneers of riveting by hydraulic power, instead of by hand, was Archibald McMillan & Son, Dumbarton. The riveting of a keel in the 1880s is illustrated.

Welding first came into use, to a limited extent, during the 1914-18 war. The first all-welded ship to be built in Britain was a 150 foot (46 metre) long coaster, the *Fullagar*, which came from the Birkenhead yard of Cammell Laird as early as 1920. As with all new things, welding was regarded with a degree of suspicion and there was certainly some justification for this. Welding causes local heating and expansion of the parts being joined. When the welded area cools it can become highly stressed and cracks may develop as a result. The positioning of the joints, and the sequence in which they are welded, both play important roles in minimizing these problems. Inevitably it took designers some time to learn the new ways and shipyard workers had to learn a whole new trade.

The first all-welded ship built on the Clyde was the *Robert the Bruce*. Together with its riveted sister ship, the *Queen Margaret*, it was built in 1934 by Denny's for the Queensferry passage. Denny's had acquired the operating rights to the ferry and took the opportunity to compare welded and riveted construction in two otherwise identical vessels. If there had been any problems the ship was near at hand for inspection and rectification, and as it had been built for their own account there would not have been a dissatisfied customer to deal with. The use of welding was greatly expanded during World War II, especially in the United States where it made possible the large-scale production of the famous Liberty Ships. Within a few years of the end of the war welding had become almost universal.

In recent years an increasing amount of work has been carried out by the prefabrication of substantial parts of the ship under cover and away from the actual building berth. In fact this change was almost a necessary consequence of the adoption of welded construction. With suitable handling equipment, large sections can be pre-fabricated and as the work proceeds they can be turned so that as much of the welding as possible is done from above, the easiest and best way. In well-equipped modern ship-yards, such as Kvaerner Govan, very large sections of the vessel are built under cover and then brought together on the berth. This reduces the length of time for which the ship occupies the building berth from a year or more to a few months. Although it was not unknown to launch a ship completely fitted out and ready for sea, it was normally just the bare hull which was launched and all the things necessary to make it into a useable and habitable ship were added subsequently. It is now common practice to fit out these large prefabricated sections as far as possible before they are moved onto the berth, thus reducing the time spent on fitting out after the launch.

Ideally, the whole shipbuilding process would be carried out under cover, and up to a certain size of vessel this is done. Yarrow Shipbuilders at Scotstoun use covered berths for building naval

Cunard's record-breaking transatlantic liner, Campania, *under construction at the Govan yard of the Fairfield Shipbuilding & Engineering Company. The Campania and sister ship Lucania (shown on the front cover) went into service in 1893.*

Right: *The bow frames, 31 December 1891.*

Above: *The frames from inside the hull, 31 December 1891. This shows several of the portable furnaces used to heat the rivets by which the various parts of the ship's structure were fixed together.*

Above: *Ready for the launch, 8 September 1892.*

Left: *The two triple-expansion engines, each of 15,000 horsepower (11,190 kilowatts). They are shown erected in the ship-yard's engine works, arranged one behind the other. When installed in the ship they were side-by-side, each driving a pro-peller via a long shaft.*

Crane installed in 1943 at the shipyard of Charles Connell & Company, Scotstoun, Glasgow, to handle prefabricated welded sections.

vessels. The advantages of covered berths are obvious and in the past, wooden ships were sometimes built under cover. In the mid nineteenth century the firm of Tod & MacGregor created two covered, gas-lit, berths 316 feet (96 metres) long by 148 feet (45 metres) wide. These were probably the only covered berths on the Clyde at this time used for the building of iron ships. Unfortunately they were blown down in a gale and not replaced.

The early yards constructing wooden vessels had little in the way of fixed equipment. The basic requirements were access to water, materials and labour. Given these, a wooden ship could be built almost anywhere. A 'shipyard' might therefore be created specifically to build one vessel and subsequently leave little or no trace of its activity. By the early part of the nineteenth century, when larger wooden ships were being built in some numbers, permanent shipyards were established but most had few sizeable items of equipment. With the coming of iron a shipyard became permanent. Shipbuilding firms might go out of business and the occupier change as a result, but the site usually remained a shipyard. Machinery of steadily increasing size and weight was brought into use. There were steam-powered machines to cut the angle-iron for the frames, shape the plates and punch rivet holes. By the 1880s riveting was done by hydraulically-operated machines wherever possible, despite the high cost of installing the plant necessary to provide a power supply throughout the shipyard. Electrically-driven machines came into use in the twentieth century. Larger plates became available from the steelworks and these were welcomed by the ship-

Many things which go into a ship are bought in by the shipbuilder. This 1901 advertisement shows some of the engine and boiler fittings available from one specialist.

builders because they reduced the number of riveted joints necessary, but cranes of greater lifting capacity were needed to handle them. Now there are large prefabrication sheds and, as indicated above, sometimes the building berths themselves are covered. Much use is made of computer-controlled tools to cut and shape the pieces of steel which will be welded together to form the completed hull. It is all a far cry from the transient wooden shipbuilding site of two hundred or more years ago!

Shipbuilding has always been something of an assembly industry. Even in the days of sail, the sails and ropes, among other things, usually came from outside suppliers. The amount of sub-contracting varied, with some of the larger shipyards having their own engine works and perhaps workshops in which the furnishings for the accommodation were made. However, extensive use was, and still is, made of sub-contractors and there are specialists making everything from the main engines and auxiliary machinery such as winches, steering engines and refrigerating plant, to small items such as navigation equipment, life-jackets and lamps.

The Leith shipyard of Hawthorn & Company in the late nineteenth century. SLA

6 With the Benefit of Hindsight

Scottish shipbuilders were world leaders in the nineteenth-century. The world market for ships has expanded enormously since 1900 and especially since the end of World War II, but the shipbuilding industry in Scotland, and indeed Britain as a whole, has not been able to take advantage of this growth. It has not even been able to maintain anything like past output levels despite the very much greater demand. In world terms the British shipbuilding industry is now insignificant and a pale shadow of what it once was. If things had been managed differently, could there still have been a significant industry today?

Depending on their point of view, some would blame the owners and managers for complacency and unwillingness to adopt new methods and invest in new equipment. Others would place the blame at the door of the workers and trades unions, with the seemingly endless disputes over demarcation and other matters. There is no denying that there was much complacency throughout the industry. However, shipbuilding was not unique in having difficulty in dealing with serious competition after a long period of market domination. The relationships between management and workforce certainly left much to be desired and no doubt this state of affairs helped to divert attention from the threat posed by the growing shipbuilding industries in Europe and Japan. However, with the benefit of hindsight, it is clear that there were other factors at work.

The Clyde became a great shipbuilding river in the nineteenth century largely because the area offered cheap iron and low labour costs, coupled with the presence of a number of innovative and gifted engineers and businessmen. Despite the failure of individual shipbuilding firms the industry was still growing and there were people willing to invest in it. Until the outbreak of World War I, British shipbuilding, of which the industry on the Clyde formed a very large part, dominated the world market for ships. Both world wars stimulated demand in the short term but made innovation in the design of the ships and in the development of the yards difficult. Particularly after World War II, when the boom lasted long enough for it to give the impression that it might be permanent, production now was much more important than planning for the future. A major problem, started by the first war and completed by the second, was the almost complete severance of the financial links which many of the Clyde shipbuilders had built up with the shipowners. Indeed a lot of the shipowners had themselves gone out of business. An almost guaranteed source of orders had thus dried up. The type of ship required was changing, and changing to the detriment of the Scottish industry. Because of developments in air transport, the passenger ships in which several of the most important yards had a special expertise were

The old way: Hand riveting of frames at Campbeltown shipyard, c1900. SLA

no longer in demand. The ships which were in demand, ever larger oil tankers and bulk carriers, had become too big to be built in any existing yard. Ironically, there is now once again a significant demand for passenger ships in the form of large roll-on, roll-off ferries and cruise ships but there is no longer a British yard capable of building them. The brand new or totally rebuilt yards in Sweden, Germany, Japan and later Korea became able to supply better ships, sooner and more cheaply, and in addition they were often able to offer better credit terms. By the time the threat became obvious it was, for most British firms, too late to compete effectively.

The modern way: the Kvaerner Govan shipyard in the 1990s, showing a massive prefabricated section which was built under cover and moved by multi-wheeled transporters to the berth on which the ship is being assembled, and from which it will be launched.

There were efforts in the late 1960s to reduce or eliminate the recurring problems caused by bad labour relations and by inter-union demarcation disputes, showing that there was a recognition of the fact that the industry had problems. But it was really too late by then. When the industry was nationalized in 1977 it was on its knees and beyond saving in anything like its existing form. One commentator, J R Parkinson, writing in 1979 about British shipbuilding as a whole, summed it up by saying that 'the industry failed, perhaps only partly through its own fault, to lay the foundations of a change from being builders of fine ships to being managers of fine shipyards'. The conclusion has to be that it probably could not have happened differently without a completely new start, with new attitudes and preferably on a new site. The attempt to change methods and attitudes at Fairfield (Glasgow) Ltd from 1966-1968 was showing some signs of working but being drawn into the turmoil that was Upper Clyde Shipbuilders did not help matters. One would like to think, though, that the progress made then played some part in making possible the survival, as Kvaerner Govan, of the Fairfield yard as the only remaining British builder of sizeable merchant ships.

PLACES TO VISIT

Scotland built ships for the world and Scottish-built ships sailed wherever there was water to float them. The result is that material relating to the history of the shipbuilding industry, including preserved vessels, is to be found all over the world and not just in Scotland or even in Britain. The *Queen Mary*, now at Long Beach, California, is well known but there are other important ships in places as far apart as Rotterdam and Honolulu. There is space here to list only a few museums, individual ships and archive sources. Priority has been given to those in Scotland and a few in England have also been included. Information on ships preserved elsewhere can be found in the *International Register of Historic Ships*, by Norman J Brouwer (Anthony Nelson Ltd, Oswestry, 1985).

Aberdeen: the local shipbuilding industry is one of the topics dealt with in the recently opened *Maritime Museum*.

Dumbarton: the building containing the *Denny Ship Model Experiment Tank* of 1883, with its equipment, is now a branch of the Irvine-based Scottish Maritime Museum. Outside the *Experiment Tank* building, there is the first marine engine built by Robert Napier, in 1823 for the PS *Leven*. For material relating to Denny's see also Greenwich.

Dundee: at the *McManus Galleries* there are models, tools and documents relating to shipbuilding in Dundee. The 1824 frigate *Unicorn*, preserved in Victoria Dock, illustrates Robert Seppings' method of using iron to stiffen the structure of a wooden ship. Also preserved nearby and open to visitors is the Dundee-built research ship *Discovery* (1901) used for Antarctic exploration by Captain Robert Scott.

Edinburgh: the *Royal Museum of Scotland* has material relating to shipbuilding and marine engineering and additional items will be displayed in the new *Museum of Scotland* which opens in November 1998.

Falkirk: *Callendar House Museum* has shipbuilding material, including records relating to the Grangemouth Dockyard Company.

Glasgow: the *Museum of Transport* has a large collection of ship models and some documentary material. Particularly important is the material relating to Robert Napier. Records of many Clyde shipbuilding firms are held by the *Glasgow University Business Records Centre*. The Port Glasgow-built sailing vessel *Glenlee* (1896) is preserved at Yorkhill Quay and the paddle steamer *Waverley* (1947) is based in Glasgow when not operating further afield.

Greenock: the *McLean Museum* has material on local shipbuilding.

The paddle steamer Iona, *built for the Glasgow to Ardrishaig service of David Hutcheson & Company by J & G Thomson. This was at the time of the American Civil War and the ship served on the Clyde for only one summer season, that of 1863, before being sold as a blockade runner.*

Greenwich, London: the *National Maritime Museum* holds the technical records of William Denny & Brothers, of Dumbarton, and other material relating to Scottish shipbuilding. The Dumbarton-built clipper ship *Cutty Sark* (1869) is preserved in dry dock.

Irvine: various ships and small craft, including the Sunderland-built composite clipper ship *City of Adelaide* (1864) and the Kirkintilloch-built 'puffer' *Spartan* (1942), are preserved at the *Scottish Maritime Museum*. There are also marine engines, examples of shipbuilding tools and a collection of documentary material. The massive engine works building from the Linthouse shipyard of Alexander Stephen & Sons has been moved to Irvine and will be used to display the collections. See also Dumbarton, above.

Kirkintilloch: documentary material relating to shipbuilding on the Forth & Clyde Canal is held by the *William Patrick Library*.

Loch Katrine: during the summer months the steamship *Sir Walter Scott*, built in 1900, provides pleasure sailings on the Loch.

Port Glasgow: a full-size replica of Henry Bell's *Comet* is displayed in the town. It was constructed in 1962 to mark the one hundred and fiftieth anniversary of the building of the original.

Portsmouth: completed in 1860 and 1861 to the same design, *Warrior* and *Black Prince* were the first British sea-going armoured warships. *Warrior* was built on the Thames and *Black Prince* by Robert Napier & Sons on the Clyde, at Govan. *Warrior* is preserved afloat at Portsmouth Dockyard.

Southampton: preserved afloat and in seaworthy condition, with Southampton as its base, is the twin-screw steamship *Shieldhall*, built at Renfrew as a sewage sludge carrier for Glasgow Corporation. Although built as late as 1955, this vessel is essentially of nineteenth century design. It is now of great historical importance as a very rare surviving example of a Scottish-built ship with triple-expansion steam engines.

FURTHER READING

ABELL, Westcott *The Shipwright's Trade* first published 1948, reprinted Greenwich 1981.

ARCHIBALD, Janette *Alloa, the Port, Ships and Shipbuilding* pamphlet, Alloa c1992.

BOWMAN, A I *Kirkintilloch Shipbuilding* Strathkelvin District Libraries, Kirkintilloch 1983.

BURTON, Anthony *The Rise and Fall of British Shipbuilding* London 1994.

DICK, Michael *The 4.15 to Cartsdyke! A Tale of Two Shipyards:- Scotts' and the Greenock Dockyard* Bishop Auckland 1993.

HIND, J A *Ships and Shipbuilding* London 1959.

KIRKCALDY MUSEUMS *Shipbuilding, the Maritime History of Kirkcaldy District* pamphlet, Kirkcaldy 1994.

LYTHE, S G E *Gourlays of Dundee, the Rise and Fall of a Scottish Shipbuilding Firm* Dundee 1964.

MOSS, Michael S and HUME, John R *Workshop of the British Empire* London 1977.

NAPIER, David Dehane (ed) *David Napier, Engineer, 1790-1869, An Autobiographical Sketch with Notes,* Glasgow 1912.

NAPIER, JAMES *Life of Robert Napier* Edinburgh 1904.

OSBORNE, Brian D *The Ingenious Mr Bell* Glendaruel, Argyll 1995.

POLLARD, Sydney and ROBERTSON, Paul *The British Shipbuilding Industry 1870-1914* Cambridge, Mass. 1979.

POLLOCK, David *Modern Shipbuilding and the Men Engaged In It* London 1884.

SLAVEN, Anthony and CHECKLAND, Sydney (editors) *Dictionary of Scottish Business Biography Vol I* Aberdeen 1986; includes a number of the leading shipbuilders, among them Peter Denny, W T Lithgow, James Lithgow, William Pearce, Charles Randolph, Henry Robb and W B Thomson.

WALKER, Fred M *Song of the Clyde* London 1984; with information on the many shipbuilding companies and an extensive bibliography.